I0814261

Intro to Chinese

Bela Davis

中文
zhōng wén

Abdo Kids Junior
is an Imprint of Abdo Kids
abdobooks.com

Abdo
INTRO TO LANGUAGE
Kids

abdobooks.com

Published by Abdo Kids, a division of ABDO, P.O. Box 398166, Minneapolis, Minnesota 55439.

Abdo Kids Junior™ is a trademark and logo of Abdo Kids.

Printed in the United States of America, North Mankato, Minnesota.

102023

012024

Consultant: Haley Chau

Photo Credits: Getty Images, Shutterstock

Production Contributors: Teddy Borth, Jennie Forsberg, Grace Hansen

Design Contributors: Candice Keimig, Colleen McLaren

Publisher's Cataloging-in-Publication Data

Names: Davis, Bela, author.

Title: Intro to Chinese / by Bela Davis

Description: Minneapolis, Minnesota : Abdo Kids, 2024 | Series: Intro to language | Includes online resources and index.

Identifiers: ISBN 9781098268282 (lib. bdg.) | ISBN 9781098268985 (ebook) | ISBN 9781098269333 (Read-to-Me ebook)

Subjects: LCSH: Chinese language--Juvenile literature. | Informal language learning--Juvenile literature. | Language and languages--Juvenile literature. | Bilingual books--Juvenile literature.

Classification: DDC 418.00--dc23

Table of Contents

Chinese is the language of China. Let's learn some words!

Chinese

English

(Guide to tone sounds on page 23)

tone signs: ā á ǎ à

Asia
N
W
E
S
China
Pacific Ocean

一
yī
one

二
èr
two

六
liù
six

七
qī
seven

三
sān
three

四
sì
four

五
wǔ
five

八
bā
eight

九
jiǔ
nine

十
shí
ten

十一
shí yī
eleven

十二
shí èr
twelve

十六
shí liù
sixteen

十七
shí qī
seventeen

十三
shí sān
thirteen

十四
shí sì
fourteen

十五
shí wǔ
fifteen

十八
shí bā
eighteen

十九
shí jiǔ
nineteen

二十
èr shí
twenty

蓝色
lán sè
blue
黑色
hēi sè
black
橙色
chéng sè
orange
黄色
huáng sè
yellow
颜色
yán sè
colors

白色
bái sè
white
红色
hóng sè
red
紫色
zǐ sè
purple
绿色
lǜ sè
green

你好
nǐ hǎo
hello

再见
zài jiàn
goodbye

早上好
zǎo shang hǎo
good morning

晚安
wǎn'ān
good night

请
qǐng
please

谢谢
xiè xiè
thank you

是的
shì de
yes

不
bù
no

家人
jiā rén
family

妈妈
mā ma
mom

爸爸
bà ba
dad

妹妹
mèi mei
younger sister

弟弟
dì dì
younger brother

姐姐
jiě jie
older sister

哥哥
gē ge
older brother

外婆
wài pó
mother's mother

外公
wài gōng
mother's father

奶奶
nǎi nai
father's mother

爷爷
yé ye
father's father

鳥
niǎo
bird

动物
dòng wù
animals

貓
māo
cat

狗
gǒu
dog
鱼
yú
fish

地方 dì fāng – Places

房子
fáng zi
house

学校
xué xiào
school

公园
gōng yuán
park

海滩
hǎi tān
beach

汉语拼音

Pinyin

tone guide

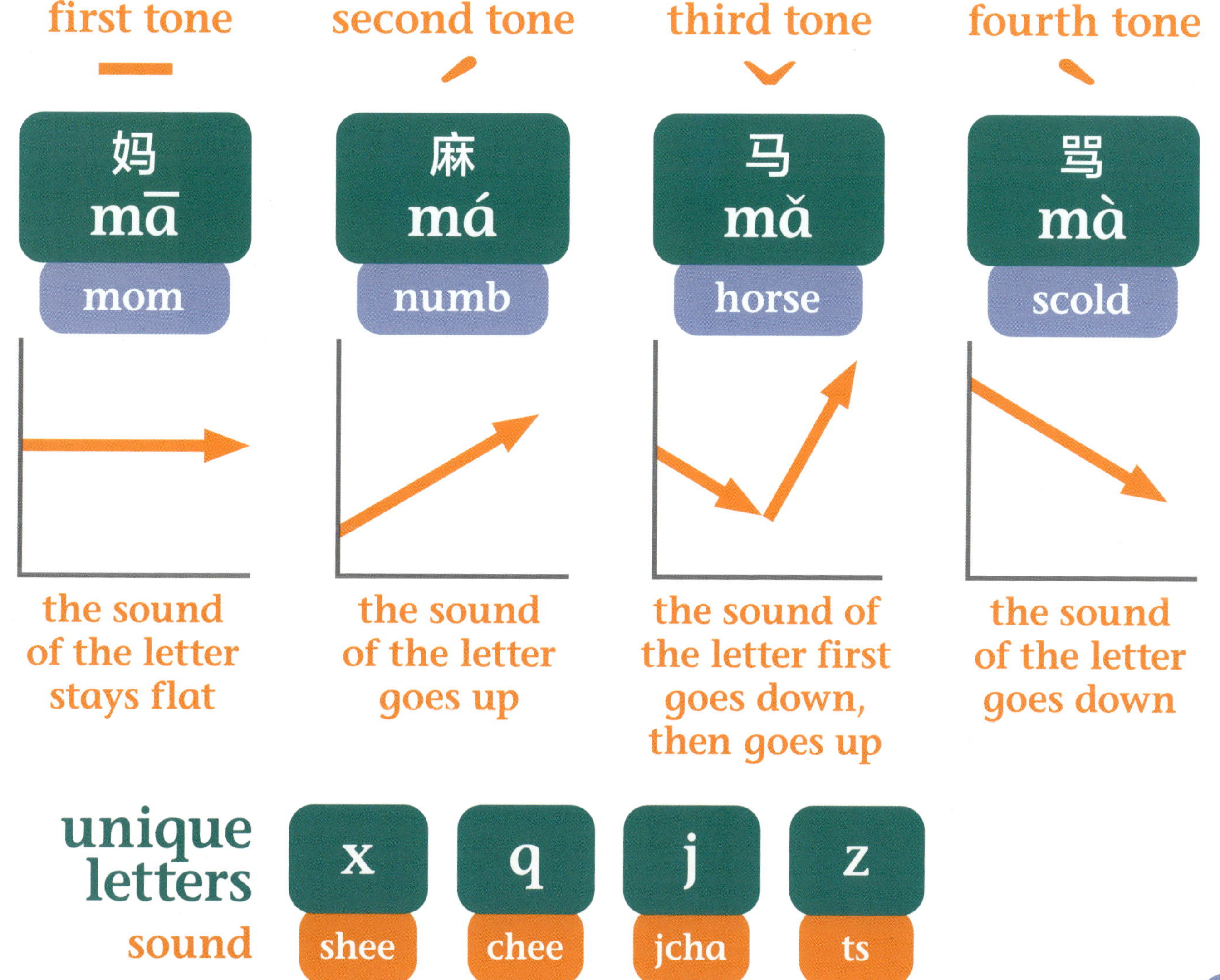

Index

Visit **abdokids.com** to access crafts, games, videos, and more!

Use Abdo Kids code

IIK8282

or scan this QR code!